WILDLIFE WONDERS

Why do birds have feathers?

And other questions about evolution and classification

W
FRANKLIN WATTS
LONDON • SYDNEY

First published in 2014 by
Franklin Watts
338 Euston Road
London
NW1 3BH

Franklin Watts Australia
Level 17/207 Kent Street
Sydney
NSW 2000

HS IBSN 978 14451 2807 8
Library eBook ISBN 978 14451 2813 9

Dewey 598

A CIP catalogue record for this book is
available from the British Library.

Series Editor: Julia Bird

Packaged by: Dynamo Limited

Picture credits

Key: **t**=top, **b**=bottom, **l**=left, **r**=right

Cover: Eric Isselee/Shutterstock, Steve Byland/Shutterstock; p1 Eric Isselee/Shutterstock; p3 Steve Byland/Shutterstock;
p4 **t** S_oleg/Shutterstock; p4 **b** Linda Bucklin/Shutterstock; p5 **tr** DM7/Shutterstock; p5 **b** Natursports/Shutterstock;
p6 (duck) Tanawat Pontchour/Shutterstock; p6 (pheasant) Tom Reichner/Shutterstock; p7 (grebes) Pim Leijen/Shutterstock;
p7 (kingfisher) tanoochai/Shutterstock; p7 (loon) Michael Cummings /Shutterstock; p8 **t** Alucard2100/Shutterstock;
p8 **b** Andrea Ricordi/Shutterstock; p9 **t** Konrad Wothe/Minden Pictures/Corbis; p9 **b** Ryan M. Bolton/Shutterstock;
p10 **t** Dynamo; p10 **b** Tracy Starr/Shutterstock; p11 **t** Beneda Miroslav/Shutterstock; p11 **b** Christopher Kolaczan/Shutterstock;
p12 **t** Eric Isselee/Shutterstock; p12 **b** John Carnemolla/Shutterstock; p13 **t** Mark Carwardine/ardea.com; p13 **b** Christian Musat/
Shutterstock; p14 **t** Tim Laman/National Geographic Society/Corbis; p14 **b** BMJ/Shutterstock; p15 **t** Wildnerdpix/Shutterstock;
p15 **b** Hans + Judy Beste/ardea.com; p16 **t** Dynamo; p16 **b** AdStock RF/Shutterstock; p17 **t** Fredy Thuerig/Shutterstock;
p17 **b** JP Chretien/Shutterstock; p18 **t** Dynamo; p18 **bl** Eduardo Rivero/Shutterstock; p18 **br** Mike Truchon/Shutterstock;
p19 **t** Larry B. King/Shutterstock; p19 **b** Tracy Starr/Shutterstock; p20 **t** Autumn's Memories/Shutterstock; p20 **b** Autumn's
Memories/n/Ardea; p21 **t** dragon_fang/Shutterstock; p21 **b** bikeriderlondon/Shutterstock; p22 **t** Pal Teravagimov/Shutterstock;
p22 **b** Sokolov Alexey/Shutterstock; p23 **t** Daniel Alvarez/Shutterstock; p23 **b** Eric Isselee/Shutterstock; p24 **t** zizar/Shutterstock;
p24 **b** Robert Kelsey/Shutterstock; p25 **t** Delmas Lehman/Shutterstock; p25 **b** Elliotte Rusty Harold/Shutterstock; p26 **t** Grant
Glendinning/Shutterstock; p26 **b** Elliotte Rusty Harold/Shutterstock; p27 **t** Kevin M. McCarthy/Shutterstock; p27 **b** Jean Paul
Ferrero/ardea.com; p28 **t** Steven Blandin/Shutterstock; p28 **b** Gl0ck/Shutterstock; p29 **t** Mark Carwardine/ardea.com;
p29 **b** M. Watson/ardea.com; p30 **t** Arto Hakola/Shutterstock; p30 **b** Eric Isselee/Shutterstock

Printed in China

Franklin Watts is a division of
Hachette Children's Books,
an Hachette UK company.
www.hachette.co.uk

Every effort has been made by the Publishers to ensure that the websites in this book are suitable for children, and that they contain no inappropriate or offensive
material. However, because of the nature of the Internet, it is impossible to guarantee that the contents of these sites will not be altered. We strongly advise that
Internet access is supervised by a responsible adult.

Contents

What is a bird?

Birds are **vertebrates**. They are warm-blooded, so they can keep their body temperature steady whatever the weather. Birds have beaks and lay eggs, but it is their covering of feathers that sets them apart from all other types of animal.

Birds are the most widespread vertebrates on Earth. Pigeons, for example, have adapted to live in most habitats, from tropical forests to busy cities.

How birds evolved

Most scientists believe that birds evolved from small, **theropod** dinosaurs. The earliest birds had teeth and long, bony tails, like **reptiles**. They also had feathers, but not all of them could fly.

A modern ostrich looks similar to Mononykus, a theropod dinosaur that lived 70 million years ago.

Terror birds

Imagine a bird more than three metres tall that weighed 500 kg and could swallow a dog whole. Phorusrhacos was a giant, flightless bird that could run at up to 50 kph. It was one of the terror birds that were the top **predators** in South America for millions of years.

Early birds

Archaeopteryx was once thought to be the earliest bird-like dinosaur, but a Chinese feathered dinosaur named Aurornis, which lived 160 million years ago, has recently claimed the title of oldest known 'dino-bird'. These **Jurassic** creatures are thought to be the link between dinosaurs and modern birds.

This is a fossil of Archaeopteryx, a flying dinosaur that lived 150 million years ago.

Phorusrhacos was a huge terror bird with a fearsome bill.

Classification of birds

There are more than 10,000 different **species** of birds. They are divided into about 30 groups, but experts often disagree about which birds belong where. The main groups are listed here.

Perching birds

This huge group is made up of about 5,500 species. It includes many common garden birds, such as robins, thrushes, crows and blackbirds.

Ostriches, rheas, emus cassowaries and kiwis

This group of large, flightless birds included the huge elephant birds, which became extinct in the 18th century.

Ducks, geese and swans

These long-necked birds have evolved to float and swim. They have webbed feet and their feathers are adapted to repel water.

Chickens, pheasants, turkeys, grouse, quails

The **ancestors** of these ground-feeding birds may have lived alongside the dinosaurs. They are found all over the world and some are farmed for their meat.

Owls

Most owls are solitary, nighttime hunters. Their excellent hearing and night vision enables them to find prey in the dark.

Hawks, eagles and vultures

Most of these birds are **raptors** and have hooked bills for tearing flesh. Some feed on **carrion** and a few eat fruit.

Flamingos and grebes

Although flamingos and grebes look quite different, scientists have recently discovered that they share certain characteristics.

Pigeons and doves

Pigeons and doves feed their young on **crop** milk, which is produced by the lining of the crop and looks like cottage cheese.

Parrots, macaws and cockatoos

These colourful and intelligent birds are found in tropical and sub-tropical regions. Some species can imitate human speech and other sounds.

Waders, gulls and auks

Most members of this group live close to water. They include sandpipers, avocets, oystercatchers and puffins.

Kingfishers

These brightly coloured birds have large heads and long bills. Some specialise in catching fish, but others eat insects, mammals and even snakes.

Loons

Loons are freshwater diving birds that live on lakes in northern parts of the world. They use their dagger-like bills to spear their food.

Hummingbirds

Hummingbirds are only found in the Americas. The tiny bee hummingbird, which has a wingspan of just 3.25 cm, is the smallest living bird.

Pelicans, herons and spoonbills

These birds have webbed feet. Many have unusual bills that are specially adapted for catching slippery fish or other underwater prey.

Woodpeckers

Woodpeckers have strong, pointed bills for boring into trees and long, sticky tongues for grabbing insects from holes.

Penguins

There are 18 species of penguin and they are not only found in cold climates – some live in Argentina, Chile, Australia, New Zealand and South Africa.

Evolution of flight

Scientists cannot agree how flight evolved. As birds' dinosaur ancestors grew larger feathers, these may have lifted the speedy little hunters into the air when they ran. Alternatively, the dinosaurs may have climbed trees and learned to fly by gliding down.

A flock of scarlet and white ibises take flight.

Why fly?

Flight uses a lot of energy, but it allows birds to catch flying prey, such as insects, and to escape from predators. By taking to the air, birds are able to cross mountains and oceans. This means they can travel long distances in search of the best feeding grounds.

Flying allows birds to live in places that other animals cannot reach. This rocky island is a safe nesting site for puffins.

Record-breaking flyers

The fastest bird is the peregrine falcon, which reaches an incredible speed of more than 300 kph as it swoops to catch its prey. Flying slowly is also an impressive feat – American and Eurasian woodcocks both fly at just 8 kph during courtship displays. The bar-headed goose is a regular high flyer at an altitude of almost 6,500 m and a Ruppell's vulture collided with a plane at an altitude of 11,277 m.

The peregrine falcon is the fastest predator in the animal kingdom.

The frigate bird has a huge wingspan of more than 2 metres, but its skeleton weighs the same as two large chicken eggs.

Lightening the load

Anything that takes to the air needs to be lightweight, but powerful. Flying birds solve this problem by having hollow bones, while their large hearts provide their flight muscles with a rich supply of blood.

Why do birds have feathers?

The ancestors of modern birds probably developed feathers to keep warm and to display to mates. Birds that do not fly, such as the ostrich, still have feathers, so they are clearly not just used for flight.

Barbs branch out from the shaft of the feather.

Shaft

Hooks link together to create a strong, but lightweight, structure.

Shaft

Scientists think that feathers evolved from scales that rose from the skin like bristles.

Birds have up to 25,000 feathers and they spend hours each day preening them.

Preening

Most birds have a preen gland near the base of their tail, which produces an oil that keeps feathers flexible and waterproof. Preening removes dirt and **parasites** and straightens the feathers so they perform well during flight.

A peacock displays his magnificent tail to impress a peahen. Her feathers are quite dull by comparison.

Fancy feathers

Male and female birds often have different **plumage**. Males usually have the most colourful feathers, which they can use to impress a female. Some birds have head crests that can be raised to attract a mate or to make a bird look bigger when confronted by an enemy.

Staying hidden

Some birds, especially those that nest on the ground, have patterned brown and grey feathers that blend into their surroundings. This **camouflage** means that they are less likely to become easy prey as they sit on their eggs. In winter, some birds lose their colourful plumage so it is easier for them to hide from hungry predators.

This ptarmigan is turning white to match its snowy winter habitat.

Flightless birds

Birds that cannot fly are thought to have evolved from flying birds. When birds have enough food at ground level and are not at risk from predators, they often lose the ability to fly. Most flightless birds live south of the equator.

The flightless kiwi is the national symbol of New Zealand. Its wings are so small, they are invisible under its feathers.

Big bird

The ostrich is the world's largest living bird. A male can grow to 2.8 m tall and weigh more than 150 kg. Although it cannot fly away from danger, the bird is a fast runner and uses its powerful legs to defend itself. A kick from one of its sharp-clawed feet can kill.

Ostriches can run faster than a horse. They use their wings for balance and steering.

Unique parrot

The kakapo arrived in New Zealand millions of years ago, when the only other inhabitants were birds and bats. With no need to fly, this **nocturnal** bird became flightless. When humans arrived, they and their pets hunted the kakapo for food. Combined with its slow breeding rate, this brought the world's only flightless parrot close to **extinction**.

The kakapo only breeds in years when trees fruit heavily, making it one of the slowest-breeding birds.

Penguins have black backs and white fronts, so when they are swimming they are camouflaged from above and below.

Superb swimmer

Penguins look funny on land, but they are perfectly adapted to life underwater. Their wings have evolved to become strong flippers, which power the streamlined birds through the sea, and they have heavy, solid bones that help them to dive. Emperor penguins have been recorded swimming at a depth of more than 550 metres for up to 20 minutes.

Mating and nesting

Male birds often put on an impressive courtship display to prove to females how strong and healthy they are. A peacock's tail fan is a well-known example, but birds of paradise put on an equally spectacular show of dances and poses that can last for hours.

When a female approaches, the male bird of paradise spreads his black feather cape around his face and flips up his blue-green breast shield.

Treasure trove

Most bowerbirds do not have fancy feathers, so the males build a structure of twigs, called a bower, and decorate it with brightly coloured treasures to attract a female. These may include flowers, stones and pieces of plastic or glass. Female birds choose their mate after inspecting a number of bowers.

This bowerbird has chosen blue as the theme for his bower.

Master builders

Oropendolas and weaverbirds both build hanging nests, usually suspended from tree branches. Oropendolas live in large groups with a **dominant** male, who mates with most of the females, while male weaverbirds use their nest-building skills to attract a partner.

Oropendolas often build their nests in trees where hornets live, to scare away any predators.

Incubator birds make giant compost heaps and bury their eggs inside them to keep them warm. Their chicks are able to run and chase prey within hours of hatching.

Making a nest

Nests protect the eggs and **nestlings**. They vary a lot depending on a bird's habitat. Some are in trees, holes or burrows, out of the reach of most predators, while others are a simple scrape in the ground. Some birds do not have a nest at all – the male emperor penguin, for example, balances the egg on his feet and keeps it warm inside a flap of skin.

Raising a family

Eggs are laid by female birds and each contains a single chick. **Clutch** sizes range from one to about 17. Eggs must be kept warm, so in most cases a parent bird sits on them once they have all been laid. Small eggs can hatch within two weeks, but a swan's eggs take almost six.

The now-extinct elephant bird of Madagascar laid an egg that weighed more than 12 kg.

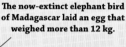

The bee hummingbird's eggs are no bigger than peas.

Egg sizes vary according to the size of the parents. The extinct elephant bird laid eggs that were 160 times larger than a chicken egg.

Elephant bird egg, height 30 cm

Ostrich egg, height 15 cm

Mute swan egg, height 11.3 cm

Chicken egg, height 5.7 cm

Starling egg, height 3 cm

Bee hummingbird egg, height 1 cm

Nest invaders

Cuckoos and cowbirds push an egg out of another bird's nest and replace it with their own. When it hatches, the bigger cuckoo or cowbird nestling often kills the other chicks so it does not have to share the food that its foster parents provide.

This cuckoo chick is far larger than the robins that are feeding it.

Feeding the young

When the eggs hatch, most bird parents work nonstop to feed their **brood**. Seabirds catch fish for their young and raptors tear off small pieces of meat for their chicks. Many baby birds are fed on insects and other bugs. Some birds swallow food and then regurgitate it (bring it up again) for their young.

Many sea birds, including penguins, regurgitate fish for their chicks because a large fish is difficult to carry and could be stolen.

Leaving the nest

After a few weeks, most young birds have developed their wing feathers. At this stage, they are called fledglings. They are ready to leave the nest, but they still depend on their parents to bring them food for a week or two.

This fledgling blue tit is about 20 days old.

Specialised beaks

Birds' beaks have evolved into tools for eating particular foods. **Naturalist** Charles Darwin noticed that finches on separate islands in the Galápagos had developed differently shaped beaks depending on the food found there. He used this as an example in his theory of evolution by **natural selection**.

Darwin's finches developed beaks that were adapted for eating leaves, seeds, fruit, grubs and insects. One became a tool user and extracted grubs with a stick.

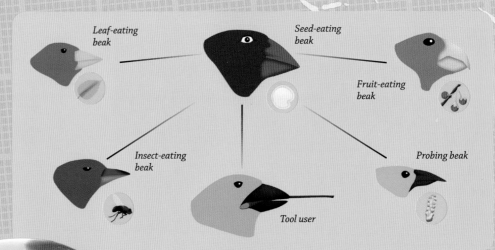

Leaf-eating beak

Seed-eating beak

Fruit-eating beak

Insect-eating beak

Probing beak

Tool user

Fruit eaters

Fruit-eating birds have big bills, so they can grasp large fruits and break through the skin.

The toucan's large beak allows it to reach fruit on thin branches that could not support its weight.

Nectar probes

Hummingbirds have needle-like beaks that are adapted to particular types of flower – some are short and stubby and others are extremely long.

Hummingbirds use their long, forked tongues to draw up nectar from deep within a flower

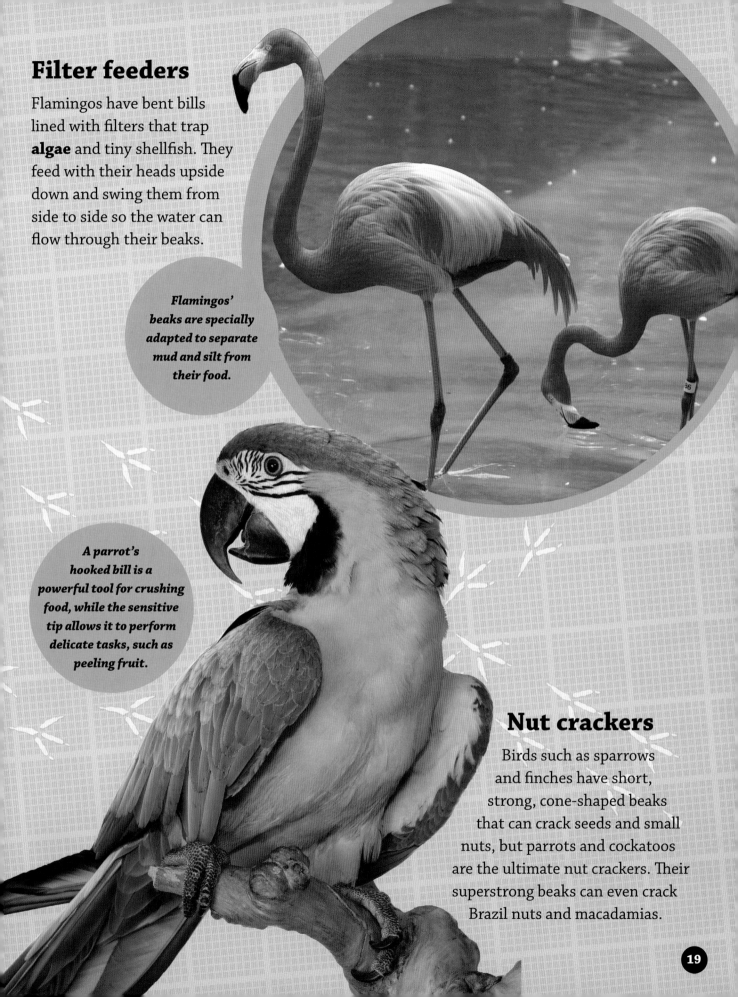

Filter feeders

Flamingos have bent bills lined with filters that trap **algae** and tiny shellfish. They feed with their heads upside down and swing them from side to side so the water can flow through their beaks.

Flamingos' beaks are specially adapted to separate mud and silt from their food.

A parrot's hooked bill is a powerful tool for crushing food, while the sensitive tip allows it to perform delicate tasks, such as peeling fruit.

Nut crackers

Birds such as sparrows and finches have short, strong, cone-shaped beaks that can crack seeds and small nuts, but parrots and cockatoos are the ultimate nut crackers. Their superstrong beaks can even crack Brazil nuts and macadamias.

Hunting and fishing

Birds that eat mammals, fish or other birds usually have superb senses to help them to catch their food. Their feet and beaks are specialised hunting tools for capturing and killing their prey.

Ospreys use their long, curved talons like hooks to catch fish just below the water's surface.

Birds of prey

Raptors use their sharp eyesight to locate their prey. They have deadly talons for seizing their victims and powerful, hooked beaks, designed for tearing flesh. Vultures are raptors that feed on carrion. As well as good eyesight, they also rely on a keen sense of smell to find a rotting carcass.

This golden eagle has caught a rabbit.

Silent hunters

Most owls hunt at night. They have large, forward-facing eyes that make the most of any available light and are adapted for judging distance. Their feathers are soft and velvety and the front edges of their wings have a jagged edge, allowing the owl to fly slowly and silently so it can take its prey by surprise.

Owls are raptors. They crush their prey between their talons, then swallow it whole.

Pelicans' beaks are very sensitive, so they can fish by touch in murky water.

Fish-eaters

Some fish-eating birds live mainly on land, while others are more at home in water and have webbed feet to help them swim. Puffins have ridges in their bills so they can carry fish to feed their young. Other fish-eaters have sharp beaks to stab their slippery prey. Pelicans have throat pouches that act as fishing nets and other birds use their beaks as filters.

Distinctive design

It is not just birds' beaks that have adapted to their feeding habits. Some birds, such as vultures, have evolved other special features to suit their lifestyles.

Vultures have evolved to have bald heads because they strip meat from bloody carcasses. Any feathers on their heads would be impossible to keep clean.

The male great spotted woodpecker has a red patch on the back of his head. His loud drumming can be heard over a wide area.

Why don't woodpeckers get headaches?

Woodpeckers hammer their heads against a tree up to 20 times a second as they use their chisel-like beaks to reach insects living in the wood. They also drum to attract mates and establish their territories. You might expect them to suffer brain damage, but the bone that surrounds their brain is thick and spongy, so it acts as a shock absorber.

How do ducks float?

Ducks spread oil from a gland near their tail over their feathers to make them waterproof. If their feathers became waterlogged, the ducks would sink. Barbs on their feathers link together to hold air in, and they have air sacs inside their bodies that keep them afloat.

When ducks dive, they squeeze the air out of their feathers and air sacs.

How do owls swivel their heads around?

Owls' eyes are fixed in their sockets and cannot move in any other direction, but they have very flexible necks with 14 **vertebrae**, compared to seven in humans. If they want to look backwards, they can swivel their heads right around, while keeping their bodies completely still to avoid alerting their prey.

Owls can rotate their heads up to 270 degrees.

23

Migration

In spring, many species of bird travel thousands of kilometres to places where they can find a good supply of food to feed their young. When summer ends, they head back to warmer regions to escape the cold weather.

Birds often fly in a V-shaped formation. This saves energy because there is less wind resistance.

How do birds navigate?

Scientists do not fully understand how birds find their way. The Sun, the stars and the Earth's **magnetic field** all seem to play a part. Birds are always evolving new routes and, in future, **climate change** may mean that some birds no longer need to migrate at all.

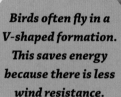

Migrating birds appear to recognise landmarks such as mountains, rivers and lakes.

Forming flocks

Birds often gather in large flocks when migrating. Extra pairs of eyes are useful for finding food – and for spotting danger, too. Birds in a large group often gang up on a predator and make noisy alarm calls, which can be enough to scare it away.

Huge flocks of snow geese migrate almost 5,000 km each year, as they travel from warmer parts of North America to their breeding grounds on the Arctic tundra.

Red knots return to Delaware Bay each May to feast on horseshoe crab eggs during the journey to their Arctic breeding grounds.

Stopover sites

Birds build up fat reserves before they migrate, but they still need to rest and refuel on the way. Stopover sites are essential and most birds return to the same spots each year. Red knots time their migration from South America to the Arctic tundra to take advantage of the horseshoe crab eggs laid on the beaches of New Jersey in the United States.

Senses and intelligence

Most birds that are active during the day depend on sight to find their food, while night hunters rely on their hearing. Some birds use touch to feel for food underwater or in the dark, and clever birds use their brains to get hold of tasty morsels.

UV vision

Some birds can see ultraviolet (UV) light and their feathers have UV patterns that are invisible to us. Male and female birds that appear to look the same may have different UV patterns on their feathers, so the birds themselves can tell the sexes apart. Kestrels are able to track the path of a vole because it leaves a trail of urine that reflects UV light.

Male blue tits have a crest of feathers that reflects UV light. Females seem to prefer the males with the brightest crests.

Touch

Spoonbills have vibration detectors on the inside of their beak, so they can feel for prey as they sweep their open bills through the water. The moment the bird feels something moving inside its beak, it snaps it shut. Owls also use touch to feel their prey. They have feathery tendrils around their bills and on their feet that act like feelers.

Spoonbills eat insects, shellfish and small fish.

Higher ear opening

Lower ear opening

Sharp hearing

Thanks to its exceptional hearing, an owl can pinpoint its prey even if it is hidden underground or beneath the snow. The ring of stiff feathers around an owl's face acts like a satellite dish. It directs the slightest rustle to the bird's ears, which are covered by the feathers of the facial disc.

One of the barn owl's ear openings is higher than the other. The minute difference in the time a sound takes to reach each ear helps the bird to locate its direction.

Brainy birds

Parrots and members of the crow family are among the most intelligent birds. Crows use tools to get food and are able to solve problems. In Japan, they drop walnuts onto the road then wait for cars to drive over them. Parrots have proved that they can understand some speech and can count up to six.

This crow is using a stick to dislodge worms from a log.

The future for birds

Birds naturally go extinct at a rate of one species every 100 years, but in the last 30 years, 21 species have been lost. Now around one in eight bird species is endangered.

The Australian Gouldian finch is seriously endangered.

Extinction

The main threats to birds' survival result from human activity. They include loss of habitat as more land is used to grow food crops, the use of pesticides in farming, climate change and pollution, such as oil spills. In addition, birds that live on islands are sometimes hunted to extinction when humans and other predators – especially pet cats – move in.

Birds, such as this swan, are badly affected by oil spills because their feathers soak up the oil.

Back from the brink

Captive breeding has saved several bird species from extinction when numbers fell too low for them to survive in the wild. The Mauritius kestrel was the rarest bird in the world in 1974, when just four were known to be left. Thanks to captive breeding there are now more than 800.

Captive breeding saved the Mauritius kestrel. Birds that were bred in captivity have now been released into the wild.

The medium ground finch was one of the finches studied by Charles Darwin.

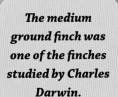

Adapting to change

Birds have evolved over millions of years and now they occupy almost every habitat on Earth, from the Antarctic to the Atacama Desert. They continue to adapt at a surprising speed. Between 1975 and 2000, the island of Daphne Major in the Galápagos suffered two severe **droughts**, which affected the size of the island's seeds. The beaks of the medium ground finches changed during this period, becoming larger or smaller according to the size of the seeds available.

Brilliant birds

Birds are some of the most spectacular and fascinating creatures on Earth. Here are just a few of the many fantastic facts about these awesome animals.

Longest migration

Arctic terns (below) migrate from pole to pole and back each year – a round trip of almost 71,000 km.

Strong stomachs

Vultures have especially strong stomach acid that kills any bacteria in the rotting meat that they eat.

Feathered giant

The extinct Madagascan elephant bird looked like a heavyweight ostrich. At 3.5 m tall it was the same height as an elephant's shoulder.

Singing star

Birds sing to attract mates and claim their territories. The brown thrasher can sing as many as 2,000 songs.

Unique flight

Hummingbirds are the only birds that can fly backwards.

Ball of bugs

There can be 300–1,000 insects and spiders in the ball of food that a swift provides for its nestlings.

Toxic feathers

The feathers of the hooded pitohui from New Guinea contain a toxin that causes numbness and tingling when they are touched.

Non-stop fliers

Swifts feed, mate and sleep on the wing. They never land on the ground, except by accident.

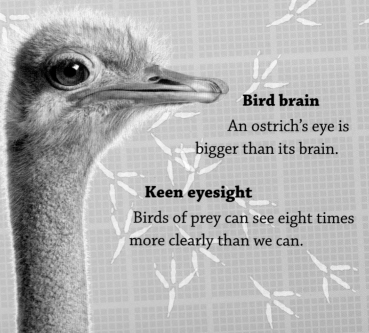

Bird brain

An ostrich's eye is bigger than its brain.

Keen eyesight

Birds of prey can see eight times more clearly than we can.

Glossary

Adapt To adjust to new conditions

Algae Very simple plants that grow in water

Ancestor An early type of animal from which others have evolved

Barb A sharp spike that faces backwards

Brood A family of young birds

Camouflage Natural colouring that allows an animal to blend in with its surroundings so it is not easily seen

Captive breeding Breeding animals in zoos, wildlife parks or other controlled habitats

Carrion The rotting flesh of dead animals

Climate change A change in the weather, often thought to be caused by human activity

Clutch A group of eggs that are incubated together

Crop A pouch in a bird's throat where food is stored before it is digested

Dominant Most powerful

Drought A dry period, without any rain

Evolve To develop gradually over generations

Extinct A species with no living members

Jurassic The period from about 208 to 146 million years ago when the largest dinosaurs were alive

Magnetic field The Earth is like a giant magnet because its core is made of iron. This creates a huge magnetic field around the planet.

Natural selection Darwin's famous theory suggests that animals with features that help them to survive will have more babies, and their babies will inherit these features.

Naturalist An expert in natural history – the study of plants and animals

Nestling A recently hatched bird that has not yet developed flight feathers

Nocturnal Active during the night

Parasite An animal that lives in or on another creature and feeds on that creature or on its food.

Plumage A bird's feathers

Predator An animal that hunts other creatures for food

Raptor A bird of prey that kills and eats other animals

Reptiles Cold-blooded animals with scaly skin. They include snakes, lizards and crocodiles.

Species A group of animals that can breed with one another and produce healthy babies, which are able to breed when they grow up

Talons Sharp claws

Theropods Meat-eating dinosaurs that walked on two legs

Vertebrae The bones in the neck and the back that form the spinal column

Vertebrates Animals that have a backbone

Index

Find out more

Here are some useful websites to help you learn more about birds and evolution.

- www.arkive.org
- http://www.rspb.org.uk/youth/
- www.wellcometreeoflife.org/interactive
- science.discovery.com/games-and-interactives/charles-darwin-game.htm
- www.nhm.ac.uk/kids-only
- http://www.kidzone.ws/animals/birds1.htm
- www.oum.ox.ac.uk/thezone/animals